What They Don't Teach You in Real Estate School

What They Don't Teach You in Real Estate School

WINNING EVERY BUYER AND SELLER

Rick Robinson and Travis Greene

© 2018 Rick Robinson and Travis Greene
All rights reserved.

ISBN-13: 9781981216307
ISBN-10: 1981216308

Table of Contents

The Story · vii

Part I: How Do We Work with Today's Buyers? · · · · · · · · · 1

Chapter 1 Stop Working with Every Buyer · · · · · · · · · · · · 3

Chapter 2 Seven Elements to Building Trust with

Your Buyers · 15

Chapter 3 You May be Showing Homes

The Wrong Way! · 27

Chapter 4 Make the Sale · 33

Part II: How Do We Work with Today's Sellers? · · · · · · · · 37

Chapter 6 Stop Working with Every Seller · · · · · · · · · · · 43

Chapter 7 Never Lose a Listing Again · · · · · · · · · · · · · · · 53

Chapter 8 Seal the Deal · 65

Chapter 9 Crap! What if the Home Doesn't Sell? · · · · · · 77

Bonus Chapter: Chapter 10 Resolving The Biggest

                Complaint in Real Estate · · · · · · · · · · · · · · · · 83

The Story

by Rick Robinson

First off, thank you for taking the time to read this book. It truly means the world to us, and we know that what we have to share in this book will be of value to you in your real-estate career. Before reading this book, we first wanted you to get to know who **we** are. How we got to where we are today. So here is our story.

In 2014, Travis and I were working at a relatively small brokerage in Rexburg, Idaho, as independent agents. We had each been extremely aggressive in our marketing, had a good following, but never felt settled that what we were doing was where we were going to stay. We always felt like there was something more. There was something that we weren't quite achieving in our real-estate careers.

One summer day, Travis walked into my office, closed the door behind him, sat down in a chair, looked at me, and said, "Hey!" Not exactly sure what was going on, I said, "Hey" back to him, and he asked, "How is it going?" I proceeded to tell him that things were fine and asked how he was doing. And that is literally how it all started.

It was a very generic, unplanned discussion, not knowing exactly "why" we were talking or where it would lead us. But you could tell that there was something on Travis's mind, and he was there for a reason. He knew that day that a conversation between the two of us needed to happen. For whatever reason, we were supposed to talk that day. But in that conversation, the idea came up of somehow doing some real-estate deals together. But it didn't go much further than that. He went back to work, and I went back to work.

Over the next couple of days, we opened more discussions of what we can do together and how we could team up and use each other's strengths. We knew that each of us had unique talents and abilities, and if we could combine them, we would be unstoppable.

Over the next few weeks, we decided to try and combine our skills and take the leap into becoming the area's *best* real-estate team. We simply knew there was a much better way to do real estate than what everybody else was doing. We didn't really know what that was going to look like or how it would work out exactly, but we certainly wanted to give it a shot. We started out by just doing listings together in an effort to see how things would go. We shared the load, we shared the effort, and we shared the paychecks that followed.

It wasn't very long after we teamed up on listings that we began to see that something was different. The way we worked together was different. The way we interacted and treated our clients was different from how other agents did. Something overall was just different. It quickly became apparent, and we knew there was more to what we were doing and what we needed to *still* do!

We then decided to officially create a real-estate team. We started meeting on a very regular basis and began working on the vision of what our team was going to be. We quickly realized that we needed to separate ourselves from the brokerage we were at, promote our team over the brokerage, and get out of the tired old box and the way things have been done over the last thirty years.

Our goal was to stand out everywhere we went in town. Our trucks already had a wrap on them, so we decided that the first thing we would do is purchase and wrap a twenty-four-foot enclosed box trailer with the new Team Greene logo. We wanted it to be big and bold, and we'd have to say that we achieved that really well! If we were going to invest the money in such a large advertisement, we wanted to promote *our brand* over our brokerage's brand, so we put our current brokerage name *very small* in the corner to be legal but keeping Team Greene Real Estate as the primary logo and name.

Shortly after, our broker became fairly upset with our new trailer and our new branding. He didn't like change, and he didn't like being left behind. However, at this point, we knew it was right, we knew it was going to be successful, and we were not going to let him change our mind. It isn't that we didn't like him, but we were trying to be something very different from what he was. And with that change came some hard feelings against us. On our end, we had tried to work with him on updating his office, updating his brand, and bringing in some technology. Despite our efforts, he was comfortable where he was, so we took things into our own hands, which he didn't like.

Our broker asked us to put the brokerage office phone number on all of our advertising as well as his logo. We said no. If we were going to be working so hard on branding and building our team, we did not want all the phone calls being routed to him or the other agents. The last thing we wanted was for all the leads and clients we generated to go to the office and being distributed among all the other agents. It wasn't going to happen.

Our broker remained upset that we were trying to be different from his brand. Change was hard for him, and he seemed to resist it. *We couldn't.* We saw the need to update, use technology, and take better care of clients. We saw the future, and we went for it. We went headfirst, never looking back, and not letting anybody block our path to where we wanted to get.

After months of our broker being unhappy with us and resisting change, we had the thought that perhaps Team Greene just needed to be its own company. But that very thought was *terrifying* to us. Just the thought of that scared us to death, but we realized that it was inevitable. We were going to have to make a leap of faith at some point if we wanted to reach our full potential.

Rick and I had secret closed-door meetings for about two months about forming our new business. We usually held them late at night with the doors locked, doing all we could to keep working going at our current brokerage while planning for our future. If we were going to make the leap of faith, we were going to do everything we could to be prepared to do it. We began creating our financial plan, our company vision, our mission statement, a full business plan, scouting potential office locations, and we developed our entire branding plan.

Toward the second month of our secret closed-door meetings, our current broker started becoming very suspicious. All of a sudden, he was dropping into our office a lot more, chatting with us a lot more. Being a little friendlier than he had before. But at this point, we were committed, and we kept creating Team Greene Real Estate under the radar.

Our entire purpose for leaving our brokerage to create a new one was to provide an *unbelievable real-estate experience to the community*. We wanted to change real estate as we knew it. We wanted to be bold in our marketing for both our brokerage and the homes we marketed, implement technology into the business, and develop a plan to offer the absolute best customer experience for the client.

Within a month of our first secret meeting, we found the perfect office space right on the busiest road in our city. We signed a three-year lease and began improvements on the building. There was absolutely no turning back at this point!

Once we started putting the office together and seeing our brand develop, we didn't want to wait much longer to make the leap of faith. While still at our old brokerage, we went and wrapped our trucks with all of our new branding and notified our broker that we would be leaving in thirty days.

Just a few days later, one very late night in December 2015, we decided to move out our desks over to the new office.

We weren't necessarily ready to start working under our new company name quite yet, but we wanted to get everything moved over so we were ready to go. That night, our broker randomly saw us moving our desks, and he immediately terminated our real-estate licenses at his brokerage, closed our e-mail accounts, and said we were done. The next day we were basically unemployed, with no way to make a living! It was *awesome*! There was no turning back. And yes, we were terrified! But this was the leap of faith we were wanting and *needing* to make, so what better way of doing it than by having no options except moving forward.

We started with *zero*. Nothing. Nada. Zilch. Our broker kept all our listings, refusing to let us take any of them with us. We had hoped it would have been different, but we understood that technically the broker owns the listings. We were *literally* living on a prayer.

Out of a dream, a vision, a necessity, Team Greene Real Estate was born.

We immediately got to work the very next morning. We didn't skip a beat. Not a day passed by. We started reaching out to everyone we knew, letting them know about our move and how we were going to provide a real-estate experience. We stuck to our plan, and we had a lot of faith that it was going to work!

We would be lying if we said it was easy. The road in front of us was steep. In the beginning of our new brokerage, times were tough. We had flown out of the safety net of our old brokerage and headed into the wind with our goals in mind and a plan in our hand.

The hard work started to pay off quickly. The word spread fast about a new brokerage in Rexburg trying to change the experience people received in real estate. We truly learned that anytime you offer *value*, you will find it doesn't take long for others to catch on and pay attention.

We began aggressively marketing our company with signage, billboard, online presence, social media, and so on, and people started saying that they saw us everywhere! Some assumed that we were one of the larger companies in town! And within just a few months, we were outselling the majority of our competition.

As time went on and we became more successful, the need to give back and help other agents was prevalent in our minds. We kicked around the idea of creating online classes, YouTube videos, and some print material to help other real-estate agents. We knew the model we had worked, and we wanted to help others become successful by following the same model. The idea started to grow, evolve, and certain key people came into our lives who made this dream a reality. Without these people to push us past where we *thought* our limits were, we would never have what we have today.

That idea grew into what is now the Real Estate Hustle Academy. We knew there were coaching programs out there and other mentorship programs, but we wanted to create something different. We wanted to help other agents create and set up what the majority of agents struggle with: the structure for a successful real-estate business. We didn't want to just merely give people marketing ideas or scripts, but we want to hold their hand in the process of creating and running an incredibly successful real-estate business. We wanted to teach people how to structure, organize, and build their real-estate business from the ground up. Everything from their back-end computer software, transaction management, branding, lead generation sources, to *how* we should work with today's buyers and sellers, how to negotiate effectively with them, and so much more. We also wanted to do it at a price agents could afford. We invite you to visit http://www.therealestatehustle.com for more information on the academy.

So this is *our* story. This is how we became who we are. This is the story that shaped us. This is the story that keeps us moving forward, and we are constantly working to improve who we are. It is the story that people know about us, respect us for, and trust us for. And now we want to help you build yours.

Enjoy the book!

Part I: How Do We Work with Today's Buyers?

Working with today's buyers is all about setting the stage for them, setting expectations, building trust, and getting them to the closing table with full confidence. But why do we call them today's buyers? For starters, the buyers we have today are certainly not the same buyers we had ten years ago or even five years ago! Nobody is walking into your office and relying on you to find them a home or asking for a book of listings. Those days are simply in the past. Today's buyers are doing their own home shopping on the Internet and their own research, looking at horribly incorrect home-value estimates, reviewing school-district ratings, exploring neighborhoods via online-mapping software, shopping Realtors like they shop for products online, reading reviews, and looking at price histories, and after they have done all of that, then they call you with a list of homes they want to see.

Realizing how different today's buyers are, we must know how to work with them, how to continually add value even when the information is at their fingertips, and how to get them to the closing table.

We are in the millennial generation for homebuyers, and older generations are quickly adopting the habits of this generation! This generation of homebuyers has grown up in an electronics-filled and socially networked world. It is the generation of "do it yourself" because the answer to any question can quickly be answered in a few clicks. So, the question is, in the world of text messages, tweets, posts, and selfies, how do we connect with today's buyers?

CHAPTER 1

STOP WORKING WITH EVERY BUYER

Here is something they probably didn't teach you in real-estate school. You should not be working with every person who comes through your door! Why? Simple. Not every "buyer" is going to buy. They can be time-consuming and take up those limited hours in your day when you could be spending them with those who are ready. Also, not every buyer will relate to you or you to them. Personalities have a lot to do with how well and how fast a successful transaction can take place! Successful real-estate agents choose their battles with buyers, and, through the pre-screening process, they work with only the most prepared and serious buyers, and then refer out the rest! Before reading this book any further, take a minute to write down who is your ideal buyer. This is critical! You must know with whom you should be working in order to maximize your time and success. So, think about who they are. What characteristics do they have? What personality type do they have? Let's do this exercise right now.

My ideal buyer:

_____
_____
_____
_____
_____

As you clearly define your buyer, you will know with which buyers you will work well and want to spend most of your time. As for those buyers you know simply won't mesh with your business practices or personality, you should send another trusted agent a referral and collect a referral fee. Sometimes it is just easier to send somebody you know and trust a referral at 30 percent and let them work with that particular buyer. It is a better use of your time to focus on those buyers with whom you can relate. Now, don't think that this is just a simple way of getting rid of clients with whom you don't want to work. You still want to add value and be of service. Sometimes that may mean "referring them" to another agent you trust, ensuring the buyers that they are in great care with that agent. It is critical to spend the most time with the people with whom you are going to work the best because you will be more productive, have greater success, and find more joy in your career! Don't make your life miserable by trying to take on each and every homebuyer! No matter how hard you try, you will not connect with the personality type of every buyer. Simply put, there are just some buyers with whom you will not work well, and you need to refer them. Period! As real-estate agents, it is normal to want to help everyone and be the hero! But sometimes your time is best spent helping those with whom you connect. As your real-estate business grows over the years, it is increasingly important that you use your time as effectively as possible, and this is one critical aspect of doing it.

Now, we all know that there are buyers who are actually ready to buy, and there are ones who say they are ready to buy but actually have not been to a bank and are just out looking for fun. In order to be successful in real estate, you need to work only with the real buyers. And the real buyers are those who are ready, qualified, and can do something about their home-shopping experience. Your role as an agent isn't to show homes; it is to sell homes.

We have a question for you. Are you currently prescreening your buyers? Are you asking them any revealing questions about what they must have or maybe absolutely don't want in a home? Have they talked to a lender? Are you taking every potential buyer who comes in assuming that they are able to buy? Before you jump in your car and show them a list of twenty homes, these are questions you need to be asking! We hate to break it to you, but everybody and their dog look at homes online just for fun! In fact, sometimes it is just a cheap date for people to go look at homes on a Saturday night! We do not want you to be the facilitator of cheap dates! You are in this business to make money, and we are going to teach you how to make the *most* money with the limited amount of time you have. So here we go!

Prescreen; Don't Interrogate

If you are not prescreening your buyers, this needs to change today! We typically will not show buyers homes until they have answered the prescreening questions correctly. Now, we understand the temptation of jumping in your car when somebody calls and says they want to see a home, but there is a much more effective way to use your time that will keep you on track for a successful real-estate career. So, whether you receive a lead from Zillow, Mom, Joe from next door, or whoever it may be, *prescreen them!* These prescreening steps are absolutely critical to take with all the buyers with whom you work in order to make the best use of your time and theirs. Now, take caution not to interrogate them on your initial phone call or at any time. If you decide to show them that first home just to get in front of them, that's OK! You can ask your prescreening questions at that time. It may be a gamble of your time, but you will quickly be able to find out whether they will become a client, a referral, or a future client when they are able to buy. Remember, you don't necessarily want your prescreening questions to sound or come across as a job interview or some sort of interrogation. Keep it light, be kind, be genuine, and ask your questions with a smile.

The Trust Feeler

Put out what we call a trust feeler. What do we mean by that? This is a statement that you will make to them to determine if a mutual relationship of trust will exist! This is *monumental* to find out before you start working with a buyer and is as simple as letting him or her know that you are excited to work with him or her. Establish the understanding that you are going to be there not to just look at homes but to actually find the buyers a home. You are the person who can make it happen for them! Start building this relationship of trust with them right away. Set the stage for what your job and your role is going to be with them. Say something along the lines of, "Our job is to not just look for homes with you, but to *find* you a home. This is what we specialize in! We are excited and anxious to help you do this!" What this does is it indirectly tells the buyers that *you* (not any other agent) are the one to help them, and it also communicates to them that you are not going to waste their time or yours by casually looking at homes. Your role as an agent is to help them find that home that will work for them and their family and seamlessly get them to the finish line. It is a "win" for all parties if that is achieved! Their response to your questions will help you determine whether or not they are serious buyers or merely window-shoppers. If they are serious buyers, they are going to be completely on board with what you just said. If they are not serious buyers, that is when it will come out. They may say something like, "Well, we are actually just kind of looking right now and are not that serious yet." With this information, you will know what to do, where to categorize them in your CRM, whether you need to refer them out, and whether you need to move on to the next client.

The Preapproval

Always, without exception, ask them if they have had the opportunity to speak with lender about getting prequalified. If they have, this is a good indicator that they are a solid buyer. If they have not, let them know that in today's market, we really need to have a prequalification letter before shopping for homes. Today's market is extremely competitive, and they need to be ready to buy as soon as the right home comes up or they will miss out! Do everything in your power to get them to your preferred lender to get prequalified. Lenders are typically able to give a prequalification letter within just a few hours, and lenders will get them headed in the right direction. Make sure to have a strong relationship with whichever lender you recommend to them because that lender will be another sounding board to encourage them to stay with you and say to them that *you* will take care of them. Make that lender part of your team! So always be sure to find out with which lender they are working. We are seeing an increased number of buyers thinking they are preapproved, whether it be from a website or a quick conversation with a lender, so *always* ensure it is a true preapproval. Always make sure to get a copy of their preapproval letter to keep on file.

The Right Questions

With all the buyers, it is important to find out what their exact *intentions* are and what their exact *expectations* are during the buying process. Again, asking the right questions will help you to discover those answers. First and foremost, don't just ask them for a preapproval amount. Find out what they feel comfortable spending. They may be approved up to $500,000, and you spend days showing them homes in that price range when, in reality, they only feel comfortable spending $380,000. You can save them *and yourself* a lot of time and frustration by discovering where they feel comfortable shopping.

Ask about their job situation. You'd be surprised how many people try and buy a home when they don't have a job, are leaving a job, or have had very little time at their job. Sometimes buyers will withhold this information during a preapproval process, but, inevitably, it will come out, and the deal will fall apart. Even if they have already been preapproved, always ask about their job situation. It tells the true story. This may seem obvious, but always ask this question.

Another question to ask is if they have already started working with another Realtor or if they are under contract with another Realtor. Wouldn't it be horrible to get to the closing table only to get a phone call from another agent saying that they had a buyer-representation agreement with that buyer?

Ask if they have identified communities or areas of interest to them. If they say that they have and they give you a list of thirty, stop them right away! Let them know that it is easy to look at too many homes or too many communities. This is far too easy to do as online search tools give way too much information. It is almost like drinking from a firehouse. Encourage them at that point to start driving around and eliminating areas that they know they won't like and come back with their list of the top five they would like to view. Drill down on what exactly they are looking for. Get specific with them. Ask them what is important in the home as far as location and neighborhood. Ask them what things they cannot live without in a neighborhood. Ask them what we should avoid in their home search. What is the most valuable thing to them in a home? You need to start digging deeper than just superficial home-search questions!

Ask them about their time frame and how soon they would like to be in their new home. Ask them if anybody else is involved in their home-buying process. Why? Wouldn't it be good to know if there is a cosigner that they have to use? Is there a grandma who is loaning them the money in cash and needs to be in the offer? Or if a parent or friend is giving them "buying advice" that you will need to correct! We need to know about these things!

Now, at this point, after you have come to an understanding of their needs, wants, and timing, just recap with them, so there are no misunderstandings and everyone is clear. Go back through the list with them. This is important for multiple reasons. It shows them that you listened, that you care, and that you are not only interested but also the right person to help them find the right home! You want to verify their wants, needs, and timing that they mentioned to you. Be the hero!

Setting the Proper Expectations

The idea of home shopping to buyers is an exciting experience! They have in their mind that they are going to find the perfect home that meets *every* expectation that they could have ever dreamed of! Right? Unfortunately, they are going to be very disappointed when they find out that "this home" with every expectation they have set in their minds doesn't exist. A fundamental part of working with buyers is helping them to understand that if they are looking for their absolutely perfect home, they will never find it! Even people who build homes quickly realize that they should have done things differently, so it is essential that you explain to your buyers what we call the *Seven-Ten rule*. This is critical. You need to set the stage and expectations from the very beginning that even though they have hopes and dreams of finding that perfect home, it may not exist.

Before we explain this rule, first let us tell you why we developed this rule. We had a wonderful client that we were working with for quite some time. They had every expectation of finding that perfect home that they always dreamed about. Being the people pleasers that we are, we told them that their dream home is out there and we are going to help them find it! When we had looked at over fifty homes with them, we were starting to get concerned. We started to see the writing on the wall. But they held us to the fact that *we told them* that their perfect home is out there and they were going to find it. Fifty quickly turned into one hundred homes. One hundred suddenly doubled to two hundred. Two hundred to four hundred. Currently, they have looked at over five hundred homes and still have not found the home they want. Don't laugh…we learned a huge lesson here! We became fully convinced that they didn't even know what it was they were looking for anymore. As a brokerage, we have had to learn from that mistake, which is why we developed this new rule, called the *Seven-Ten rule*.

For every agent at our brokerage, this is the new standard. Now, although the situation that we ran into is relatively rare, it is truly important to set realistic expectations from the very beginning! Expectations are very difficult to change once the buyers have their mind set on something, so start out on the right path with your clients. For about the last year, we have implemented this rule and the results have been incredible! We are finding families homes faster and accommodating more buyers, and our brokerage, as a whole, has been able to achieve greater success by just this one simple rule.

In your initial visit with your potential buyers, during the prescreening process, make a list of their ten must-haves in a home—the things that they feel they cannot live without. Now, even though these are going to be the ten things they feel they cannot live without, you (and the client) will quickly realize together that they can, in fact, live without all ten. Explain to them that in your years of experience selling homes, the perfect home doesn't exist. The majority of people don't find a home that meets every single one of their expectations. There is always a bit of give and take, and the clients will generally agree. Then explain to them that if we can find a home that meets *seven* out of their *ten* must-haves in a home, it is a home worth considering! Many things can be changed or modified in a home to make it a ten-out-of-ten home, but during the buying process, it is important that we set our expectations at finding a home that has seven out of the ten must-haves. The rest can be changed.

Ask them directly, "If we find a home that meets seven out of your ten must-haves, would you be prepared to make an offer on that home?" Once we explain this rule to our clients and ask for the commitment, the success rate of finding someone a home jumps to 100 percent. Why? We set the stage and the expectations for them. The reality. We are *not* showing clients fifty to hundred homes anymore before finding the right one! We are generally showing them less than five homes before they buy because they have their expectations set at a more realistic level. It is a win for the clients! A win for you! It just makes for an overall *great* real-estate experience!

In Review:

- Ask thorough prescreening questions to discover needs and challenges.
- Put out a "trust feeler" to gauge their commitment to you and to build the foundation of trust with them.
- Always make sure to get a copy of their preapproval letter ASAP. If they aren't preapproved, get them to your preferred lender immediately.
- Ask them about their intentions and their expectation for the home-buying process.
- Always ask up front if anybody else is involved in their home-buying process, such as another Realtor or a cosigner. This is vital information to know up front.
- Set expectations with your buyers up front. Explain the process to them, so there are never any surprises.
- Always explain the Seven-Ten rule to every buyer.

CHAPTER 2

Seven Elements to Building Trust with Your Buyers

Not to be Underestimated

Don't ever underestimate the value of trust in a relationship with a buyer! Just don't do it! Without this relationship of trust between the agent and the buyer, even the most successful agent out there will ultimately fail. Trust is everything in a real-estate transaction, so how do you earn it with all of your buyers? Let's find out!

The Seven Elements of Trust

Trust is both emotional and logical. And when working with buyers, you are going to run into both. It is important to understand which type you are working with, so you can adapt your approach to quickly build trust with them. On the *emotional* side, it is where you expose feelings and your true personality to people. You get down on their level. It is important to recognize how people who rely on the emotional side of trust behave. People who shop for homes based on emotion tend to make decisions faster. They often go by how they feel in their gut. These buyers like to hear you describe how from the large kitchen window, you can see your kids playing out in the yard on a sunny afternoon! Those things resonate with them. They enjoy the excitement and hype of buying a home. They like the *thrill!* As long as you can keep them excited about the home, you will probably make the sale.

It is important that you know how to connect with the emotional buyer. Adapt your speech to connect with them. Let your guard down, get on their level, and be open with them. Think with us for just a moment about Oprah. She is a figure that so many people trust because she has let down her guard and has been open to the public about her struggles and her successes in life. She has been incredibly successful in building a community of trust around her personal brand! You, too, can achieve the same success as you let down your guard, allow yourself to connect with your clients on an emotional level, and help point out features of a home that will hit that emotional side of their trust.

Now, trust on the *logical* side is all about the facts. What will my payment be? What will my utility bills be in a home that is twenty years old versus a new home? These are the buyers who will purchase *Consumer Reports* to research the appliances that come with the home to ensure they are going to live to their expected utility. These people want to know facts, and facts alone. They don't get overly attached to a home because of the colors, carpet, and layout. The more paper work they can have in their hand about the home, the neighborhood, schools, and so on, the better. They don't like or appreciate the excitement, the emotion, or the hype of purchasing a home. They want details, details, and more details. To them it is a decision, not a dream.

Is every buyer going to be 100 percent emotional or 100 percent logical? Some may argue that clients are always emotional and never logical! Well, in reality, clients are always a mix of the two to some degree. Whichever side they lean more toward is the side of trust we need to *focus* most of our efforts on. When you are home shopping with a couple, it is possible that one may be emotional and one may be logical. So you are going to have to work double time to gear your communication accordingly to generate trust with each individual.

We are going to walk you through every step *we* take in our brokerage to build trust with our clients, whether emotional or logical. We know they will work for you! The level of trust we build with our clients is real, tangible, honest, and something we value, and we want to share how we are able to get there quickly! Now, some of these steps may be things that you are already doing. But be sure to take notes on the ones that you are not doing. There are always some things that we can all improve on. Before we go any further, list five things below that you are currently doing to build trust with your clients. Then let's take a look at the seven elements we have found to work. They may be the same or different, and that's OK!

1. _____

2. _____

3. _____

4. _____

5. _____

Building Buyer Trust Element 1: Be Their Friend and Be Their Professional

Emotional: First and foremost, above anything else, be their friend. It sounds simple, but it is so critical. People want to work with people. What do we mean by that? People want to work with someone who will relate to them! Someone who they feel they can be open with. Be the person who they can have open conversations with, or give a helping hand to them when needed. Be someone with whom they can sit down and laugh! Be the person who they can take advice from. This will break down so many walls and barriers quickly. If you can achieve a friendship status with them up front, you will have won half the battle. It is not as hard as you think. Just be yourself; don't be overzealous, overmanipulating, overly egotistical, or an overly annoying real-estate agent. Get on their level. Yes, you are the real-estate professional, and you are acting as their consultant, but you can also be their friend. We typically end each transaction with our clients wanting to have us over for dinner. Seriously, it is achievable!

Logical: The logical buyers are going to want to know that they have someone on their side who is going to be their professional real-estate consultant. Be there for them to answer questions and gather details. Never make up answers to their questions. In order to achieve this level of trust, you will need to do some research about the homes prior to showings. Then quickly follow up after those showings with any additional information the clients request. Remember, they want facts! The more details you can hand them at a showing about the home or area, the happier they will be. Fluff won't cut it; details do!

Building Buyer Trust Element 2: Take Time to Answer Questions

This element is very straightforward, yet we are finding that many agents are not doing this. Take time to answer their questions! People are going to have a lot of questions during the real-estate transaction. Give them your time and well thought-out, detailed answers to their questions! Let them know that there is never a dumb question and that you are there to help them! Make a point in every e-mail communication that they *should* ask questions throughout the transaction process and that you are there to help them. This will put them at ease, resolve their hidden concerns before they become an issue, and make you the proven professional during the real-estate transaction process. Make sure to ask them at the end of each showing what questions they have that you can follow up with. The emotional buyer is going to think that you are just the nicest person in the whole world to think about him or her like that. The logical buyer is going to know that you have his or her best interest in mind and that you are going to be a reliable source.

Building Buyer Trust Element 3: Preparation

Be prepared. That's it! Period! It is so simple, yet so many agents will generally fly by the seat of their pants! It is normal! It is normal because we have shown a thousand homes, we have written hundreds of offers, and we feel we know what we are doing. But going that extra mile with preparation will go the extra miles with your clients!

Prepare before showings! Don't rely on your experience or super-Realtor powers of the past! Some buyers are more casual and rely on emotion, while others want details and specifics. Find out which you are dealing with during your initial interview, and then adjust as necessary. For the logical buyers, gather as much information as you can gather on the homes you are going to look at. Present a packet of information to them at the showings! And don't feel like this is a waste of time and paper because this is their lifeblood! Since you are now only going to be working with the most serious buyers, because of your great prescreening process, take seriously that they are worth the investment of time and a few pages of paper to blow them away with the research that you have done on the homes! This will help them to trust you that you have their best interest in mind. Be up-front, and tell them about any negative issues with the home you know about.

Don't ever, under any circumstances, try and hide anything about the home that may come up as an issue later. You shouldn't do that anyway. It is wrong professionally and morally. Always be up-front. Don't worry about blowing a sale because you brought up something negative about a home.

They will appreciate your honesty and hold you to a higher level than before! Prepare for your meetings with them. If you are going to be writing an offer with them, prepare ahead of time to have drinks ready, perhaps a snack, paper work mostly filled out and ready to complete, and show them that you are ready for the next steps to the home-buying process. A little preparation goes a long way!

Building Buyer Trust Element 4: The Good and The Bad

Bring forward good and bad information, always! Sometimes agreeing with the buyers that a home is a piece of garbage is a good thing! It will help them to know that you are not just trying to sell them any home. If there are things that they do not like about a home, it is OK to agree with them! Avoid selling them something that isn't in their best interest. It is always best to be honest with the clients instead of pushing them in a direction that you know will not deliver the outcome that they are looking for. Don't withhold bad news, but always remember to celebrate the good news! Build on their positive comments, and point out the features you know they will like or that they have already mentioned and fallen in love with. Show them you are listening!

Building Buyer Trust Element 5: Questions and Statements

Do you want to know the key to a successful real-estate transaction? Ask this simple question to every buyer you work with:

"What can I be doing better for you?" It doesn't matter if you have met with this client one time or ten times, keep asking that question persistently. What can I be doing to best help you? This will show that you truly care about the client, his or her needs, and are doing what is best for him or her. When you are showing the clients homes and you first enter the home, set the stage, and tell them, "As we go through this home, tell me what you do and don't like about it. Be open with me! It is not my home... you won't offend me! It helps me to know what you are looking for." Let them know that you don't want to push them into just any home. Tell them with confidence, "I don't care what home you buy. What matters to me is that you like it and that you can be excited to come home every night. Honestly! It could be a $5,000,000 mansion or a cardboard box. It makes no difference to me. It needs to make sense or 'we' won't let buy it!" Notice that we use the word "we." This indicates your interest in *their* good decision and buying experience. Buyers are usually very nervous, and they need your vote of confidence. Ask them how they are feeling. If they tell you that they are nervous, tell them, "Good! I would be nervous if you *weren't* nervous!" Reassure them that nervousness is normal in a real-estate transaction and that only means you care.

Building Buyer Trust Element 6: Respect Your Competition

Be respectful to your competition at all times, no matter how much you may disagree with them! Be kind! Some people think that trash talking your competition will make you seem better or make your services look better. Trash talking your competition will not only diminish the trust people have in you but will also have them wondering what you may be saying about them when they aren't around. So just don't do it!

You may find yourself in a situation with a potential client where he or she may bring up something another agent said about you! In fact, an example of this just happened to us not too long ago. We received a phone call from a family who was looking to sell their home, and they were calling several agents. As we were giving them our pitch to use our company to list their home, they mentioned that another agent, and they told me which agent it was, criticized our photography saying it was "too nice" and that it deterred traffic from the listing. Honestly, people are looking for anything these days to try and put us down because we have a very large market share! In this instance, we could have started ripping this other agent apart, their lack of sales, lack of professionalism, or many other things. Instead, our response back was, "Hmm. We really like that agent. That is really funny he'd say that! Well, let us tell you why professional photography is important to getting your home sold." We weren't going to waste our time attacking another agent. We don't ever want to be known as the agents who are looking for ways to put other agents down. Simply put, always take the high road. You will only benefit from it.

Building Buyer Trust Element 7: Own Your Mistakes

If you drop the ball on something, own up to it. Don't push the blame on to somebody else. If you forgot to answer their questions, forgot to set up a showing, or whatever else it might be, own up to it, and apologize. This will build more credibility and trust than trying to push the blame on to somebody else. They will respect you because you are showing them your vulnerability and that you are human. None of us are perfect. Mistakes happen. Own up to them! It will be fine. You need to own up to mistakes even after the sale! Here is an example: We were recently working with a young widow who was moving here from back east, and she was really going through a tough time. She had recently lost her husband after he was trenching in his yard and hit an underground power cable. She is probably in her forties, now a widow, and needed to move out to Idaho to be closer to her daughter. We cannot express to you how important a relationship of trust was with this client for her personal benefit and for the sake of moving the transaction forward confidently. We set the expectations up front, we established trust, we laughed with her, we cried with her, and, overall, we had a great time together! The home-searching process was successful and a great experience! She mentioned to us that this was just the experience in real estate that she needed.

Some time after we closed on the home, there were a few problems that came up with the house. Because she had a comfortable relationship of trust with us, she immediately reached out to us after the sale with a question she had. She remembered what we told her during the home shopping that with Team Greene there is never a dumb question! During our initial tour of the home when we were out home shopping, there was a music system playing in the home that really set a wonderful atmosphere as we walked through the home. When we decided to make the offer on the home, we had just assumed that it was included since it was built in. However, when the sellers moved out, they ended up taking the audio receiver, which made the entire system nonfunctioning. We looked back and reviewed the contract and realized that we did not specifically state in the contract that the receiver had to stay. We had all just assumed that it would. Right away, we apologized to her, we let her know that it was our mistake, and we showed up on her front door with a brand-new audio receiver and spent about an hour at her home installing it and showing her how to use it. Did we have to do that? No, we did not. We could have easily ignored her because we had collected our commission check already, and the deal was done. However, the value of keeping that relationship of trust is priceless and important to our company and us personally!

There is no better time to work on building trust with your clients than right now. Start today! Identify the areas that you know you need to be working on, make a plan, and start working on it. Remember to adapt your trust-building skills to both sides of the spectrum: emotional and logical. People express themselves based on the way they think. They will manifest their "trust-building type" through their speech, their dress, the car they drive, and so many other factors. Pay attention to these clues, and adapt your trust-building elements as necessary. You will soon learn to read people based on these factors and know how to quickly build the relationship of trust with them.

In Review:
- Be their friend, and be professional.
  - Take time to answer questions.
    - Prepare.
- Bring forth the good and the bad.
  - Respect your competition.
    - Own your mistakes.

CHAPTER 3

YOU MAY BE SHOWING HOMES THE WRONG WAY!

The Little Things Count

It seems obvious, but people cannot buy homes unless we show them homes! But, there is a good way and a bad way to show homes. You can waste a lot of time showing somebody dozens of homes that they do not like, or you can take a more effective approach and show them fewer homes and get these people to the closing table sooner! There are many things that we have learned over the years that have helped us to be efficient and effective at showing homes. Right out of the gate, we want to put the buyers on track with a process that we can follow together. This will not only build trust since we have a joint plan but also help eliminate them from wanting to see five hundred homes! Trust us on this one! A common plan of action builds that foundation of loyalty, so they don't go out and shop other agents or even feel the need to do so.

Now, there are many little things that if they go overlooked will derail your client's trust and confidence in you.

We are not going to go over all of them, such as forgetting to plan the route, knocking loudly, announcing yourself before you walk in a home or a closed door, making sure your eKey is paid in full (which has happened to us once when a credit card expired and we didn't realize it until we had a list of ten homes to show one day and the e-key suddenly stopped working!), taking off your shoes, turning all the lights off, and things like that. We are taking things a step further. Yes, the little things do count and we know that most of you are probably doing this already. But just as a friendly reminder, make sure to always arrive at the home first. Be on time! Don't park right in front of the home; make sure that spot is reserved for them. Turn all the lights on before they come in the home. And when they arrive, welcome them to the home. Literally, use the word "welcome"!

Now, this is where some people have developed some bad habits. We have found that the most effective way to show a home is not to show it! That may sound odd, right? Let us explain. First put the buyers at ease quickly, and then let the people explore the home and get to know it on their own. When you first walk them into the home, tell them to feel free to wander around, open cabinets, roll on the floor, open closets, and get a feel for the home. Remember, you are not looking for homes that *you* like. You are not the one who will live there.

As they explore the home, of course, you have to be the chaperone and make sure that they do not go in and start pulling things out of cabinets or pulling food out of the fridge and are making a sandwich. In fact, on that note, we had a home inspector inspecting one of our listings after we had a home under contract, and this family happened to have cameras inside their home. As the home inspector was walking around, the homeowners were watching him on the camera. That is what people do when they have a camera system! This home inspector opened the pantry and started *eating* their food. The homeowners were absolutely shocked as they were watching this happen! They could not believe their eyes! He was reaching into their kid's snack food and was eating away! But the best part of it was when he had a mouthful, he turned to his right and saw a camera staring him in the face! He uttered the words "oh crap" as he knew he was caught! The point is, you never know when someone is watching! Now, getting back on topic!

The best way for somebody to get to know the home is on their own! Do not be a mother hen and follow them everywhere they go! Let them self-discover the home. This helps them to talk openly about it! Even though they know you do not own the home, sometimes they withhold comments or feelings because they don't want to offend anybody! Let them talk among each other as a family! This is best achieved when you are not following them around like a baby elephant following its mom.

This does not mean that you need to just stand there, or sit in a corner, and be silent! If you know that this home has a feature that was on their "must-have list," then make sure to politely point it out. As you welcome them into the home, let them know what boxes of their "must-haves" are checked with this home! Point them out! "Guys, this home has a ton of natural light! It has the big and open windows to the backyard that we talked about!" Then, send them on their way, and let them wander around. After they have looked around, then talk with them. Ask them what they did or did not like about the home, and reinforce the things that they like. If it is absolutely a terrible home, they know it, and you know it, tell them, "OK, I agree, not a good home; let's just go to the next one."

Be Slow to Offer Your Opinion

Be very slow to offer your own opinion. If they do not like something about a home, don't jump in and say I agree! We had an example of that just the other day. We were showing one of our listings, and the homeowners had recently refinished their kitchen cabinets to a distressed, white antique look. The wife walked into the kitchen and said that she absolutely hated those cabinets! Now, we could've jumped right in and said, "Oh my gosh, me too! They look horrible!" But instead, we remained silent and did not offer our opinion, and, naturally, the husband offered his opinion! He said encouragingly to his wife, "You may not like them, but you will never be able to tell when they are dirty. And if the kids ever ding them up, it will just add to the distressing, and you will never know!" The wife agreed with him, and all of a sudden, she was able to overcome those kitchen cabinets with us not having to do a thing. Again, be slow to offer your opinion. If you need to interject your opinion and help people to see something, great! Do it! But be slow to do it. Sometimes a few moments of silence will fix the cabinets!

Don't Overdo It

Don't overdo it. Silence is OK! I was once invited to one of our listings during a showing because another agent's buyers requested that the listing agent be present to answer questions about the home. As the other agent was showing the home, I just stood back and observed. She followed them around like a mother hen. She was about six inches away from their back the entire time and did not stop talking! She pointed out every basic feature out such as the electrical outlet placement, lights, and the carpet—things that the buyers could obviously see with their own eyes. As they turned a corner, with her shuffling right behind them, I could see an incredibly annoyed look on their face. I had to chuckle a little bit because I knew that these people were just being driven nuts by this agent.

Sometimes distance, too, is OK. People need to breathe! Let them explore, and let them form their own opinions, and you be there as the consultant only! Again, this all goes back to developing the trust.

Always remember, the buyer is buying the home, not you. It has to work for *them*! Always make sure to ask them at the end of each showing if this home checks seven out of the ten boxes of home requirements for them. This will make them think. This will help them to realize that maybe the little things they did not like about the home could be overcome if the bigger, more important items were there. Don't let them focus on the "one" thing that may be wrong with the house. Affirm to them the six good things it has. You know as well as we do that sometimes one thing about a home can literally make a buyer think that the home is completely and utterly uninhabitable. Always, always, always use the seven-out-of-ten rule with your buyers to paint the true picture. You will thank us!

CHAPTER 4

Make the Sale

You will probably agree that driving around and showing homes is relatively pointless if you can't ever make a sale! So, how do we take them from showing homes to writing an offer? There are always those few clients who feel like they need to go and see just five more homes before they decide on one, just to be sure! Well, that is not the best use of time, and the more they look, the better the chance they will lose out on the one they *really do like*! This is where the expectations, building trust, and *your skills* in showing them homes and negotiating come into play. Always keep pointing out those benefits, getting on their level, and rehearsing the seven-out-of-ten rule with them. If they hit seven out of their ten, tell them to stop looking and start offering or they may lose the home! Always remember to be encouraging, be excited for them, and be open and ask them about their emotions and their feelings. Again, getting on their level is key to helping move your clients along! Often, first-time buyers will admit they are nervous! Let them know that it is good to be nervous and that it is fully expected and that you are there for them!

Help the buyer through the nervousness. That is your job! The more comfortable they feel going into it, the more likely you are to have a smooth transaction. Your preferred lender can help you with this as he or she too will meet with them and be that reassurance. Review with them everything that will happen in the real-estate transaction, and break it down step by step. Don't let there be any mysteries!

What we do for our clients is we outline the entire real-estate transaction and let them know that from the day an offer is made, they will get e-mail updates with every step of the process, so they know what to expect, where to be, and how things will work. We coach our Real Estate Hustle Academy students on this religiously, and we provide them with all the templates. We even go as far as defining real-estate terms in these e-mail updates, so they know and understand real-estate lingo. Again, you want to make them feel as comfortable as possible when making an offer on the home. Buyers want to be included and feel that they are part of the experience, that they understand and are not just along for the ride.

Go through the offer process with your buyers and the four different outcomes that may happen. Let them know that the offer can be accepted, rejected, the seller may accept another offer, or they may counter back. Explain the elements of negotiation and have them put themselves in the seller's shoes, and ask them what *they feel* the home is worth. Depending on your market and area, there may be concessions offered, reductions in the purchase price, or other local trends. Discuss those, and set the stage of the negotiation. Have this conversation with them:

"Mr. buyer, oftentimes, buyers will think that if they save thousand dollars off the list price, they are actually saving thousand dollars. Now, this is true for the sellers because every thousand dollars they come down in price is exactly thousand dollars out of their pocket. However, as a buyer, at a four percent interest rate, that is only about four dollars out of your pocket per month. That means it would take two hundred and fifty months (or twenty years) for you to catch up to that thousand dollars you feel you just saved, and most people don't even live in their homes for ten years! Knowing that, what is the best offer we can make on this home today so you don't lose it?"

You have something good to offer each of your buyers: those who are your "now" buyers and those who are your "future" buyers. Treat everyone with the same respect, friendship, and courtesy. Place them in your CRM according to their needs and time frames, and make sure to follow up. You are valuable! Your time is valuable! Your ability to help others to the finish line in their journey to homeownership is your purpose and your goal. Set the stage, create new prescreening habits today, build those relationships of trust, and start to win every buyer who comes your way. Using these techniques, there is no reason why you should ever lose another buyer again.

Part II: How Do We Work with Today's Sellers?

Could you imagine having the confidence that you could walk into literally any listing appointment and know with a surety that you would be walking away with that listing? What does this take, and how do we get there? Well, we're going to show you how! It is important that we first understand something. We all know that today's sellers have tools that they have never had before and they are incredibly empowered by websites such as Zillow, Trulia, and other such websites that give them tremendous amounts of market information. This in turn gives sellers the sense that they "have the tools" necessary to do it themselves! So, how can we, as agents, continue to add our important value to today's sellers and keep ourselves involved? How do we overcome these obstacles and have the confidence that we can indeed walk into any listing appointment knowing that we will walk out with that listing? This is a critical question we all need to ask ourselves. But a question we have the answer to!

Today's Obstacles

We have previously discussed why buyers are different in today's world, but what has the world of the Internet done to "sellers"? Why is working with sellers today different than what it has been for years and even decades? For starters, it used to be that real-estate agents exclusively held all the market data. We had it all! Nobody else had access to it! We were the kings of the real-estate market data! Now, the real-estate associations have decided to release all this information, often for free, to all kinds of consumer websites. Listings and listing information, what homes have sold for, and vital market information. Many websites have taken this valuable information that we used to hold so sacred and have published it to the world. Now, we are presented with the situation where the sellers have almost as much access to market information, comparables, and the ability to post and advertise their home online as we do! They don't need a license, they don't have to pay commissions, and they can take everything to a title company and get it done for just a couple of thousand dollars. Does that sound like a problem? Have you faced some of this opposition before? If you go to Google and type in the search bar "how to sell my house by owner," it is amazing how many mainstream companies and media sources are walking a seller through exactly how to sell a home. It's frightening! Putting the real-estate market in the hands of the public who has little to no experience in home sales, the negotiation process, marketing, finance, insurance, inspections, title work, or the several other critical aspects of real estate is *very* concerning! Yes, the protection you as an agent offer is priceless!

If you were to visit our local market in 2016, you would have seen that nearly 40 percent of all listings in our market were for sale by owner. It was absolutely insane! It was darn near depressing! It was one of the toughest years in real estate that we have had. Although the recession was tough for many, a 40 percent FSBO market was just brutal! The issue we started to run into was that the "for sale by owners" had to become part of a second MLS that we searched when looking for homes for clients! There were so many of them, and they made up such a large part of our inventory we had no choice! In fact, typically about 50 percent of homes on buyer's lists we worked with were for sale by owners! Now let's understand that for sale by owners are just as great as those who list with agents. Our concern is simply that they are taking critical matters into their own hands because technology said they can, and the risk of a serious problem is very real. Our goal is to protect the client and ensure a smooth and seamless transaction and a happy real-estate experience. Truly, I wouldn't go to YouTube and watch a video on how to perform a heart surgery, and then try it on myself! Then *why* does someone feel he or she can take the largest financial investment of his or her life and deal with it alone? It just isn't sound reasoning. To prove the point, when we would make the phone call to the for sale by owners to ask if we could show their home and that we had a qualified buyer, they would say, "Fantastic! Send us their contact information, we are for sale by owner, and we do not need an agent." *What? Really?* We really had to defend our value! And although this situation was very difficult for us and had put us in a slight panic, we knew what we had to offer was needed and there was the need to dispel the myth that just because you can means you should! This particular year in real estate really opened our eyes and our minds, so we went to work. We further defined our value as real-estate agents, set new goals, looked into the future, and came up with a plan to succeed. We had no other choice! The resistance came regularly, even daily! If we told the sellers that our buyers insisted that we help them even though it is a FSBO listing, they would simply say, "Fantastic! That is fine and dandy, but since they want you, they get to pay for you." The sellers just simply didn't understand that we were not "taking" their money, but rather we were adding to the transaction by creating security, clarity, and success.

So, the real question in today's world is *how* do we add value for sellers? How are we going to justify a 6 percent commission to real-estate agents when the sellers think they can do it by themselves? What are you doing currently to defend your worth? What is it about you that is going to sell them on hiring *you* as their real-estate agent?

Do you see the reason why you need to be prepared to work with today's sellers? This is a different world of real estate. Not only are we competing with other agents, but we are now competing with websites. It is the new way people shop, buy, and sell! So we better be where they are and know how to work with them!

We have gone to several hundred listing appointments. Out of those, we can confidently tell you there are maybe only a few that we did not win, generally due to a certain friendship or family member in the business. So, it is safe to say that we have a very good track record with what we do, and we want to share with you what makes our listing presentation so compelling, convincing, and effective, giving the seller the confidence to go with us. By the end of this section, you are going to be empowered with the tools that you need to get out there and win every listing appointment that you go to. If you follow these steps, there should absolutely be no reason why you do not walk away with a listing each time you go to a listing appointment. In fact, we have gotten to the point where we actually get very excited when we know that we are competing against other agents because we know we have a better way of assisting our sellers and we are excited to tell them *all* about it! These opportunities for us to tell our story excite us! They put us into hyperfocus and really dial in our presentation, which helps us improve each time. Implementing a positive attitude and always studying our competition keep us at the top of our game! In fact, if we know who we are competing against, you better believe before our appointment we are researching what those agents are doing and what they are not doing, and we make sure that we are doing things better!

It is incredibly important that you believe in yourself! Believe in your value! Believe that you do indeed "add value" to the real-estate transactions! If you do not believe in yourself, then *why* should that seller believe in you?

CHAPTER 6

Stop Working with Every Seller

Now, the truth of the matter is, you will most likely take the majority of all listing appointments that come your way. It is normal, natural, and how successful Realtors are wired! We just want to help everyone we can, show others our best, and overall succeed! One thing you need to do when a phone call or e-mail comes in about somebody wanting you to list their home is celebrate! And what do we mean by that? In this world of technology where the public feels they can do everything on their own by having multiple online guides and how-to videos, that client *still* called you! For some reason or another, they took the time, picked up the phone, and dialed your number! So…celebrate the fact that these people called you. Keep them on a short leash, take it as an opportunity, and do everything that you can to get an in-person listing appointment with these people quickly. Time is of the essence!

When we talked previously about working with today's buyers, we went over the importance of prescreening the buyers. Simply there are buyers out there who are serious and ready to make things happen and buyers who are not! Equally we want to make sure that we are always working with the most serious sellers. It is the very same process for these sellers as our cherished buyers. There are serious sellers, and there are sellers who actually may have no "real" intentions of moving. It is important that we prescreen our sellers because, as we have talked about before, you have limited hours in the day and limited resources, and we need to make sure that we are being the most productive with our valuable resource—*you*! Believe it or not, there are sellers out there who go to the trouble of listing their homes at ridiculous prices knowing that it most likely will not sell, but they just wanted to "test the market." This is just wishful thinking and a complete waste of time. Frankly, agents who do not prescreen sellers just like they would a buyer are going to put a lot of time, money, and effort into marketing a seller's home when in reality they will probably never ever see a commission check. Does that sound like something you'd be interested in doing? How fun would it be to work for an excavation company and agree with them to dig a six-foot deep ten-mile-long trench that takes six months or more to do only to find out it never really went anywhere. It just ended in an empty field. You never get paid, it never added up to anything of value, and it cost you money up front in tools and machinery you never get reimbursed for! Does that sound like a blast?

There are certain things that we need to do to prescreen our sellers. Working with sellers who will never make you money is not our idea of a hobby or a good time! We definitely do not encourage it. By now, you have had the chance to prescreen your buyers and have seen the benefit and the difference in how productive you are and the increase in closings you achieve. Once again, this is the same goal with sellers. And just like the buyers, we want to make sure that as you are prescreening them, it should never sound like any sort of interrogation or job interview. We want to be friendly, courteous, and very professional. Build trust at every opportunity!

When you get the phone call about somebody wanting you to list their home, very casually ask them a few questions. As you practice this skill, it will come easily and naturally. First, you will always want to thank them for the opportunity to work with them...out of the gate assume you got the listing! Then thank them for thinking of you as "their" agent to list their home! Assure them that they have made the right choice by choosing you as their agent. Casually ask them trust-building questions such as, "How long have you lived in your home?" This shows them you are interested and opens the door to more conversation about their family they raised in that home. Ask them, "Where are you moving to?" This tells more of the story of their urgency and needs, which is helpful to you in planning. Tell them you are excited to work with them and ask, "How soon can I come over to meet with you in your home?" This will tell you how serious they are and again show them you are proactive. What you're really doing is finding out if they truly have plans to move or if they are just fishing around for home values to try the FSBO approach.

If they say, "Well, we don't know, we are just looking to see what the market is doing," then a FSBO may be "coming soon to a neighborhood near you"! So go into your save-the-client mode, and tell them your story, your value, your success history, and why they need you! Once you get them to understand they cannot live without you as their Realtor, ask them for details about their home, so you can come prepared to the listing appointment with comparables of both listed homes, closed homes, and paper work ready to sign! Always go to the listing appointment with the mind-set that you are there for a purpose and you are not leaving without the listing. Now, this does not mean you be pushy or in any way take on the "do-what-it-takes" mentality to get the listing before you leave. There is no place for a pushy arrogant Realtor. We just mean, if you're planning to get the listing before you get there, you probably will!

In Review:
- Ask trust-building questions.
- Relate to their needs.
- Prescreen.
- List.

Recall our discussion on trust from the previous section. Sellers generally operate on the statistical and analytical side of trust, whereas buyers are more emotional. Since statistics are important to sellers, when you are on that initial phone call, let them know how successful you have been in the area! It's OK! There is a difference between bragging and informing. Let them know how many homes you have sold recently! If you haven't sold very many just yet, but we know you will, share with them a success story of a family you helped or some other encouraging experience to show your value. Let them know that they're going to be in very good hands with you and that you have full intentions of going to work for them and getting their home sold. Be that bold from the very beginning. We believe to "always begin with the end in mind." From the very beginning, visualize yourself with that listing, with that seller, and at the closing table with buyer and seller. Go into this with that kind of confidence.

As soon as you set that listing appointment, go over with them what to expect. Let them know that, within the next couple of hours, they will receive an e-mail with a marketing plan for their home. Set the stage for how you work, your organization, and how motivated you are to sell their home. Now we can guarantee that the other agents that you were competing against will most likely not have a marketing plan in place and ready to go for that home before the listing appointment. But you will!

Confidence! This initial phone call is the key! You can win or lose a listing in less than five seconds if you do not start right! So what is the *right* way to start your initial conversation with a seller? First the don'ts. *Don't* sound weak. *Don't* sound scatterbrained. *Don't* sound clueless. *Don't* sound uninterested. If you are not completely dialed in on the initial phone call, they will already have the preconceived notion that you may not be a very good agent, and they will have already checked out before you get their names. Now the *Do's*. *Do* be confident. *Do* be good at resolving concerns and question. *Do* be where you are when you're there, and stay focused on them! *Do* stay on the subject! *Do* know your local area, so you can talk confidently to them about where their home is. This is critical and shows your professionalism. Basically, your job for the next few seconds is to put them at ease, gain their trust, prescreen them, and set the appointment. You can do this! Just practice and role-play to get your own pattern and mojo down. They say that practice makes perfect, but I believe perfect practice makes perfect!

On the topic of confidence, this is something I've had to work on over the years. It is not something that comes very natural to many people, and it didn't come naturally to me. But it is *very* possible to acquire. I recall a time when I was in a situation where my life literally depended on my confidence. When I was going to college, I decided to get my private pilot's license. This had always been a dream of mine. So, one day, I drove down to the local airport, started walking around, and started asking for a flight instructor. I happened to meet somebody who knew one, called him, and the very next day I flew an airplane for the first time with that instructor. I was hooked! Between going to school full-time, working a part-time job, and working on my pilot's license, it took me about six months to get my license. I remember the joy and excitement I felt the day I received it. It was a major accomplishment for me. But now that I had my license, I realized that everything was in my hands. There is not going to be an instructor by my side to coach me in difficult situations. *I* had to do it! It was up to me; however, I felt I was now more confident than ever before and would be able to handle any situation that I encountered. Before I knew it, I was put to the test!

One day my family was visiting in town, and I took them on a flight up to West Yellowstone, Montana. The flight was beautiful. No wind, blue skies, smooth air, and incredible sites. We flew over lakes, over streams, over mountains, and over rivers. It was beautiful! We landed in West Yellowstone without any incident. We got off the plane, walked into town, and had a nice lunch. Overall we simply had a great time and a great day! As we were walking back to the airport, the wind out of nowhere started howling! There were twenty-seven mph sustained winds with gusts up to forty mph. My plane was fully loaded, full of fuel, very heavy, and was going to be difficult to get off the ground with the combination of very warm weather, high-elevation, and an extreme crosswind that I had never dealt with before. I was worried to say the least! To top it off, I happened to be in an airplane that did not have a steerable nose wheel, which makes things much more challenging as it acts just like a caster wheel on a shopping cart. This meant that my only control of steering the airplane down the runway was with my rudder and the individual brake pedals. This is very unique setup, compared to most airplanes, and was hard enough to steer in calm weather.

Well, we needed to get home. We all jumped in the airplane. As I prepped the instruments and engine for takeoff and called to the tower, the plane was sitting there shaking and rocking back and forth because of the wind (and so was I). At this moment, I realized that the life of my family literally depended solely on my confidence level, calm thinking, and execution of what I knew I not only needed to do but was capable of doing. I knew I was a good pilot, but in moments like this, it is easy to start to doubt your skills and yourself. I had to literally push through all those doubts, remember the skills that I had been taught, and see the end in sight of us getting off the runway without any incident. Making it back to our destination was the goal! I don't think my hands had ever been so sweaty! As I increased the power, we started to roll down the runway. The forward role quickly turned into a zigzag across the runway! I knew everything depended on me to get us off the ground! We seemed to zigzag forever! But I fought against the wind and eventually got us off the ground and safely into the air. With my hands still sweaty, we arrived back to our destination, and the trip was a success. What could have derailed me mentally, creating a potentially tragic situation, became a triumph and a success. Confidence is what got me through that difficult and scary situation. Confidence can get you through anything you fear in your career.

Again, I understand that it can be scary and nerve-racking to talk to potential sellers and going on these listing appointments. Practice! Practice your confidence as if your life depended on it! Confidence isn't required when we are in our comfort zone; it is required when we are out of it! I have often reflected on the moment when my life depended on my confidence, and when I get in situations where confidence is needed, I know that if I could get through what I did on that runway, I can become better enough to do anything! Kill any negative thoughts that may enter your mind. Challenge yourself to push past your fears! Conquer them, and tame those thoughts and feelings that keep you from being your true and best self! By the end of this book, you will have built your confidence to a new level that will help you to break through barriers that have been holding you back!

You need to believe in yourself. Acquiring this trait will help you achieve self-discipline and the desire to grow! Desire results in greater productivity in learning what you need to know, so you can confidently talk to your sellers and *win* every listing! If you are prepared, there is no need to fear! Practice with a coworker, practice with a spouse, or practice with a friend! Practice simply will give you the confidence that you need to handle any situation when you take that initial phone call for a potential listing. If you do not believe in yourself, they certainly will not believe in you.

We encourage you to write out a script or an outline for how this phone call should go, something that you can memorize and keep ingrained in your mind. Something that you can look at often or carry with you that you can make a quick reference to if you are on the go. We encourage you to do this today!

CHAPTER 7

Never Lose a Listing Again

Have you ever considered how an opera may turn out if everybody showed up without a costume or without having done any preparation? Or a Formula-One race where nobody laid out the course or they forgot to put gas in the car? How fun would the play be or which direction would you go on the track, or how would you get down the road! All would be a complete disaster for sure! Yes, perhaps very funny to watch…but the end result would not be what you desired. Equally, you simply cannot go to a listing appointment unprepared. You need to have your tools ready, confidence level boosted, and prepare to go in there and *win* that listing!

You would not believe how many agents we have talked to who do not have a listing presentation or marketing plan to share with their client. Do you have a listing presentation? If you do, is it relevant for today's sellers? Does it show how you are *adding* value to them in a world where they think they can do it on their own? Is it so *convincing* that they would feel foolish to not use you? If not, we are going to make sure in the next few minutes that your marketing plan is on par for working with sellers in the twenty-first century.

Now, for those of you who do not have a listing presentation at all, it is OK. We are going to work on building one right away.

Now, you really only need to build it one time because, as you e-mail it to clients via your CRM or mail service, it can be automatically customized to that particular client. Simple and effective! If you do not have a CRM set up, this is another major part of the Real Estate Hustle Academy that we teach. It is well worth your time and effort to go through the ten-week academy to get your business structured in such a way that you can scale it. Please go today and visit http://www.therealestatehustle.com.

In your initial phone call when you were prescreening the sellers, you will inform them that you will be sending them over a listing and marketing presentation via e-mail. There are a few very specific things that you need to have in this e-mail, which are your prelisting presentation *and* your marketing plan. Sending these two items *before* the listing appointment will ensure them that you come across as confident, knowledgeable, prepared, and professional and that they would be absolutely crazy to ever go with an agent different from you!

So let's build this convincing e-mail. This marketing plan. This *tool* that is going to help you win every listing! Below we are going to outline every element this needs to have.

Element 1: Express Gratitude

Entrepreneur Magazine wrote an article back in 2014 about the power of a thank-you.[1] They said, "There is a free, readily available resource that you probably underuse. It can change moods, increase engagement, and make people work harder. It's a simple 'thank you.' Saying those words cost nothing, yet we can be stingy with their application." They go on to quote the author Mark Goulston, who wrote the book *Just Listen: Discover the Secret to Getting through to Absolutely Anyone*. The author said, "If you're deeply grateful to someone who's done an exceptional favor for you, you need to express that emotion by going beyond the plain words 'thank you' and instead offer a Powerful Thank You. When you do this, your words will generate strong feelings of *gratitude*, respect, and affinity in the other person." Elements of this "thank-you" that need to be present are as follows:

BE SPECIFIC: Don't just tell them "thank you." Tell them *why* you are thankful.

PERSONALIZE IT: Luckily, your CRM or e-mail campaign software will help you to personalize their e-mail automatically! But thanking them by *name* means much more than just a general "thank you."

BE AUTHENTIC: Don't make it feel forced! You really *should* be genuinely thankful for this opportunity. Express that! Remember, any real-estate client can spot a fake from a mile away!

---

[1] https://www.entrepreneur.com/article/220770

Element 2: Introduction Letter

Write an introduction letter about you and your company. People want to know about you! So help them get to know *you*! If you work on a team, tell them about your team! And make sure to tell them that teams often have more success than the individual agent and why. Share with them your brand. Share with them your creation story and why you exist. Put in a few of your branding elements to help them feel part of your culture. And in this introduction letter, instill in them the confidence that they are choosing the *right* agent! Always take the chance to assure them that they have chosen the right agent and that they are in good hands with your company—*you*!

This is an appropriate place to insert a video introduction of yourself! Let them get to know you and the team that they will be working with. Keep it short and concise but effective and memorable! Remember, you have less than five seconds to win or lose them!

Element 3: Your Marketing

Describe clearly what you do to market homes. This is truly the main reason why they hire a real-estate agent now. Like it or not, one of our greatest values in the eyes of the homeowner is our marketing ability. And this is where you *really* need to shine! Right now is a great time to take inventory with what you are actually doing to market homes! Are you doing anything different than other agents? Are you just following along with the crowd? What is the best way to find out? Whatever path you need to take by all means. Find out!

Start stalking the other agents! See what your competition is doing! We are always watching our competition because we want to make sure we are *always* one step ahead of them. Seriously!

Where is your photography at? We absolutely cannot settle in today's world for anything less than amazing photography. You may need to start hiring a professional photographer and pay them $100 to $300 to photograph the home. Presentation is everything! If you are not 100 percent confident in your photography skills and don't have access to a nice camera or Photoshop, hire someone who does! If you would like to save the money of hiring a photographer, take our course on real-estate photography, www.therealestate-hustle.com. We can train *anybody* to take professional photos and even get you all the right equipment to do it. This "marketing" course is well worth its weight in gold. You must heavily emphasize the importance of photography in your listing presentations. Let them know that between twenty and forty million people visit Zillow on a monthly basis and the number-one feedback from consumers is that they want to see pictures. Pictures speak more than a thousand words when selling a home; they speak a million! High-quality pictures alone can make all the difference with two competing homes in a neighborhood. It may even sell for more because presentation is everything! Make sure to include a link to your photo gallery of homes you have previously listed, show people your great work, your ability, and how you take the *time* to put their home at the top of the shopping list!

Video and videography! Right up there with the importance of professional photography of a home is a professional video of a home and a video walk-through. Explain to your seller how you are one of the only agents who will put the required time into your listings that it takes for them to sell. Also, that a professional video walk-through of their home is your unique touch, so people can get to know their floor plan and home features and feel as though they have walked through their home before they ever arrive! Explain to them that this will help bring only the most serious buyers to their home, because they will have already seen the home ahead of time, but it weeds out any buyers who may come to tour the home only to find out they don't like the floor plan. Again, give them links to videos that you have put together. Show them what you have done! If you don't have any, put some together! Go find a vacant home, and make that first video! Video provides a buyer the experience of vision, color, sound, feeling. Those things one cannot get from a still photo.

Talk about your social-media campaigns! Assure them their home is going to be on Facebook, Twitter, Instagram, YouTube, and also any community Facebook pages that may exist in your area. You will do a Facebook live-stream video with a market preview. You will make a beautiful post about their home with photography and a link to the video walk-through. We live in a social world! One cannot go thirty seconds without seeing someone glued to their phone looking at social media or some kind of digital ad. That is where people are, and that is where their home *needs* to be!

Just a quick side note, when we do our initial listing prescreening, we are just giving them little bits and pieces of our listing presentation. We are not going to outline absolutely everything in this e-mail to them. We want to save some things for the actual listing presentation. We want to make sure that this e-mail is relatively short enough for them to actually read it and not just delete it but detailed enough that they know that you mean business. Effective and balanced!

Element 4: Client Reviews

Send them a link to your client reviews, and explain why reviews are so important. Tell them that just like Yelp and TripAdvisor for travelers or Amazon for products, consumers have a chance to go on and write reviews for real-estate agents. Ask them to think about the last time they bought a pair of shoes or researched the next book that they're going to read. They probably began with consumer reviews. Why? Because reviews are candid. They're not published by the company promoting the product. They are not fluffed up with marketing lingo and meaningless words. Most importantly, they are the words of people just like you. These reviews are very important for consumers to read before they choose an agent. So get those reviews from everyone you meet, have done business with, or had something to do with in real estate. Even if you were just a friendly agent who answered some questions for a buyer or seller, ask them to leave you an encouraging review on the experience! Just get them, and make *sure* they are all five star! Send your clients and prospective clients to the link to your Zillow account where you have been gathering your reviews or perhaps other sources where you may have received reviews. Invite them to leave you a review, and then *thank* them for their support!

Remember to actively be asking for consumer reviews! We cannot express enough the importance of this. Do not ask people to read your reviews if you do not have any! Makes sense, right? Make sure you have a minimum of five to ten solid reviews if you are going to give them a link to read them. Remember to ask in every moment and in every situation for a review. Please do not forget to carry your review cards with you, handing them to anybody you show a home to. Review cards are business cards with a bang, and we always carry them with us so that we can hand them out to clients at any time! When the time is right and the iron is hot, hand them a card and ask for that review!

- Eighty-four percent of people trust online reviews as much as a personal recommendation!
- Seven out of ten consumers will leave a review for a business if they're asked to, so *ask*!
- Ninety percent of consumers read less than ten reviews before forming an opinion about a business. Be at the top of that list, and make sure the reviews are good!
- Fifty-four percent of people will visit the website after reading positive reviews, so make your site compelling!
- Seventy-four percent of consumers say that positive reviews make them trust a local business more—where do you rank? How can you be at the top of that list? Get there!

Element 5: Competitor Reviews

After they have read your reviews, invite them to read the reviews of any other competing agent that they may be interviewing. Be confident that you are going to have more reviews and better reviews than your competition. Now, if you have not built your review portfolio yet, then maybe you should wait until you have more reviews. Always make sure that you have more than they do and that they are better. Reviews are difficult to get, but we know you can absolutely do it. We have been able to achieve over seventy reviews on our Zillow account in the last year. So can *you*!

Set goals to get a certain number of reviews per week. Our goal is to get one to two reviews per week. It may not seem like much, but they add up quickly. Set a goal right now, and create a strategy to fulfill that goal! A Realtor without reviews is like a car without gas. A pencil without lead. Or a boat without water. You will not receive the traction that you need to succeed in real estate without consumer reviews.

Element 6: Brag a Little

It is time to brag just a little bit! Show them *how many* homes you have sold and the people you have helped in your local area! Nobody wants to go to a heart surgeon who doesn't have a good history or track record. I wouldn't! The same goes for sellers. They prefer to work with an agent who has a history of getting homes sold. According to statistics from the National Association of Realtors, sellers tend to choose an agent with a proven track record and experience. So prove your track record. Again, remember that we are dealing with the analytical and statistical side of your mind with sellers. They want details. Show them exactly how many people you have been able to help, and let them know that you are excited to add their home to that list. Now again, agents who are just starting out may not yet have a strong track record or list of home sales. So brag about your competency of the market or your understanding and ability to properly market a home. Share something of value that sets you apart!

Element 7: Excitement

Reiterate once again that you're excited to go to work for them. Let them know that you will get started right out of the gate to properly market their home and to get it sold for the most amount of money and in the quickest time possible. Try not to promise three days or two weeks as that may not always happen. But encourage them all the right elements will be in place for the quickest sale possible. Tell them you look forward to meeting with them and you look forward to being their agent!

So, why is it important that we send this e-mail? For starters, we can guarantee that your competitor will most likely not send an e-mail like this. They will not set the stage and begin building a foundation of trust with the sellers. They will usually show up, give their spiel about why they are different by usually saying things like, "What makes me unique is I actually care about my clients and work hard." Guess what? Things like that just don't really fly anymore! They are hiring a professional marketer and consultant to get their home sold. Let them know that you are very serious about your job, have been successful in your job, and will bring success to them!

A quick tip. Before your appointment, if a day or so has passed by, make sure to confirm your appointment with the sellers. Call them or shoot them a quick text to make sure that the appointment is still set with them. Begin rehearsing what you will say to the sellers in the listing appointment. Practice in the mirror if you need to! Start building a confident appearance. Think about it; how do you think the agent will do who says, "Well, yeah, I guess I can sell your home; I'll come take some pictures, put it on the MLS and stuff, and we can see what happens." Compare that to the agent who comes in there and says, "Just look at my track record! I am in the business of selling homes, and I am one hundred percent confident that we will get yours sold!" Much shorter, more confident, and far more effective! Confidence is the key when working with sellers. They want to know that they are in good hands. Remember, they are paying you very good money. We know how crazy some of these commissions can get! You want to do everything that you can to show that you are actually earning what they are paying for.

Things you can do:
Take some time to prepare market statistics for their neighborhood. Pull up active listings, recently closed properties, and calculate what the absorption rate has been for that area.

Finally, make sure you look presentable. Make sure you are clean cut, wear clean clothes, and are presentable. There is a plumbing company that advertises that they are the "smell-good plumber." Be the smell-good Realtor! We hate that we even have to say it, but even just yesterday, we showed up to open one of our listings, and the agent showing it was in pajama pants and had a scraggly beard. Your presentation can make or break the confidence of your client within seconds. If you act like a professional, you'll *be* a professional!

In Review:
- Always add value.
- Tell them why they need to be using you.
- Always let your excitement shine through.
- Dress for success.

CHAPTER 8

Seal the Deal

The big day has arrived, and you are ready to go to the listing appointment! This is the time to show off your skills, seal the deal, and put the sellers at ease. Come prepared with your statistics, comparables, and know everything about current inventory and sales in your market.

When you arrive at the home, make sure to arrive about fifteen minutes early. As you were waiting, pull out your phone, go live on Facebook, and do a video promoting this person's house! Let people know that it is not on the market yet, that it is a market preview, but that it will be on the market very soon, and tell them what a great home it is! Let people know that if they want an exclusive peek at this home before it goes on the market, to give you a call! This is something that will come into play a little later on in the listing appointment. Trust us! But take initiative to start marketing the home right off the bat! Don't waste any time. Be proactive.

Remember, once again, confidence is the key. Do not underestimate yourself, your talents, or your abilities. You are a rockstar agent. You have something to offer! You are going to offer something that most other agents can't offer. What it all boils down to is this, how well you can deliver your listing presentation. No matter how much detail and effort you put into your presentation, if your delivery of it is short of a bloopers reel, your chances of success are few! But, by following all the steps that we go through in our program, we can guarantee that you're going to be offering more than your competition, doing so with more confidence, and winning more listings than ever before. So, do not underestimate your value! Be bold, be confident, but make sure you stay on the level of your client. Don't over run the show, but don't fall asleep at the wheel!

Start off right away by thanking the sellers for the opportunity to come to their home, and make sure to compliment them several times on their home. Point out the features you know they take pride in. This shows that you are observant, are paying attention, and care! Let them know that you realize that there are many agents out there, but explain to them *why* you are different. Ask them this question: "Before we get started, do you have any questions for me?" They may start right off and ask you how you will market their home. That's great! You know they are interested in "getting to the point"; follow their lead and move forward. Don't be so regimented that if your plan isn't carried out exactly how you planned it, you fall apart. Go with the flow, and get on their level and wavelength. If the conversation is up to you to start, then tell them, "Well, let me show you what I have already done to market your home," and get that conversation started. Always break the ice where you can and build that trust level first, and then fill in the blanks based on their attitude, observance, and interest. Sometimes you need to be that chameleon and change as needed! This is when you pull out your phone and show them your Facebook live video, talking about their home and how it will be on the market soon. This will show them that you have already taken initiative, are proactive, and are ready to get to work. In fact, you already have! Show them that you already posted on Facebook and are trying to generate leads to get their home sold. Knock their socks off. *always...overdeliver!* Especially when you're *not* asked to!

Have a conversation with them that every single agent puts the home on the same MLS, on all the same home-search websites, on their personal websites, and most likely on social media. Nobody has a secret place where they are advertising homes that makes them sell better. What it boils down to is how well an agent can *market* the home. Let them know that you are the master of marketing! Before you get any further, ask them if they had the opportunity to read the marketing proposal that you had e-mailed over to them. If they said yes, tell them wonderful! And briefly run through some of the points of the e-mail. Point out to them the importance of professional marketing for their home. It used to be that agents would only do professional photography for high-end homes. Tell them that you do not discriminate against any home and that every home deserves equal treatment for representation online. Ask them, did you know that listings with professional photos typically sell for more money? Not only that but they sell quicker. Ninety-two percent of homebuyers use the Internet as part of their home search. Photos are an absolutely critical factor. It can determine the price of the home, how quickly it sells, and whether it sells at all. The first impression to online buyers is absolutely critical! Having professional photography and a beautiful representation of their home is far more important than a listing description these days. In fact, the majority of people do not even read listing descriptions anymore! It can also affect their perception of the home prior to seeing it. A good photograph will have a positive emotion associated with the home. Emotion is the number one trigger of the affluent buyer, so use it to your advantage. A good photo can speak not one thousand words but one million words!

Let them know that you will use proper equipment, the home will be properly lit, and you only take high-resolution photos of the home. Let them know that while every other agent is out there taking pictures with their smartphone, you are willing to put in the effort or pick up the expense of doing professional photography for their home. Yes, professional photography is an added expense, but when you put a home on the market, you're competing against lots of other properties. If those properties are highlighted with attractive, beautiful photos and yours isn't, you're going to have more trouble getting potential buyers through the door. This could cause your home you have listed to sit on the market longer than it otherwise would.

Remind the seller, between twenty and forty million people visit Zillow on a monthly basis. And this is just *one website!* The number-one feedback from consumers who are looking to purchase a home is that they want to see pictures. Which is why you will deliver!

If you had a tablet with you, show them some samples of your photography. Show them samples of your competitor's photography. Now again, we have to be careful not to talk poorly of our competition, but really, all you are doing is showing without malice what your competition is doing versus what you are doing. It is really no different from the battle between Ford and Chevy and each company showing what the other company is doing to try and make its product look better.

Let them know that not only are you going to do beautiful photography of their home; you are also going to do a wonderful video walk-through of their home so that potential buyers can literally go on a virtual tour of the home and know if they like it before they even schedule the appointment. Explain to them what this does! It is to prescreen buyers so that we don't waste anybody's time with people who come to the home and may not end up liking the floor plan. By the time somebody sets foot in their home, they will be qualified by the bank, they will have seen the beautiful photos, and they will already be taking a tour of the inside of their home. If they go a step further and set an appointment, then we already know they are going to be a relatively serious buyer. Let them know that we weed out the riffraff because it is a waste of everybody's time, especially theirs.

Pictures by Far Outweigh the Description of Their Home

If you have been through our Real Estate Hustle Academy, don't be afraid to share with them that you have been through one of the nation's best real-estate training programs! That is one more leg up that you have over your competitor.

Now, the time has come to go overpricing their home with them. This is always the biggest struggle in listing appointments. We always know that sellers want to get the absolute most out of their home. Most of the time, it is ridiculous what they want! So, this is where you come in, as their professional real-estate consultant, and help them to understand that you're not just here to list their home, but you are here to *sell* their home. A technique that we always use is the concept that there are four prices to every home! There is the price the *seller* thinks it is worth, the price the *buyer* thinks it is worth (which is probably the most important), the price the *appraiser* feels it is worth (also important for loan purposes), and the price that the *county assessor* feels it is worth. And what we have to do is find a happy medium that will please everybody. Ask them, "Mr. seller, if you were a *buyer* looking at your home, what would you honestly pay for it?" Put them in the shoes of the buyer so they can understand that the buyer is the person we need to appeal to! There is no use appealing to themselves! We need to appeal to the people with the checkbook!

Now, since you have come prepared with comparables that are currently listed on the market and ones that have closed, start to review these with them. Start with the listings that are currently on the market in their neighborhood that are similar in size, square footage, and features. They need to see what their immediate competition looks like. Let them look at what their neighbors are doing. Chances are that they may even have been in these homes and will know exactly what they are up against, which will help you in pricing their home. The discussion you want to have with them is that all these prices are wishful thinking until the home actually sells. Remind them that although these homes are listed at this price, they have *not sold* for that price. A home is only worth what a buyer is willing to pay for it. Now, after you have gone through the active listings, pull out your recently sold listings and show them what homes are *actually* going for. History is the best gauge of value! Show them the price per-square-foot breakdown of each home. Now cost per square foot is only a gauge. The same size home across the street in the same neighborhood may be worth more than your clients' if it has been updated with granite countertops, two-tone paint, new carpet and appliances, and so on. So again, do your homework, and don't just price a home by the square feet. Know the competition! Then let them know that there are three options that we can choose to price their home:

> **OPTION ONE:** Pushing the envelope and listing at the top of "fair market value." Let them know that this will produce the fewest showings and will rack up the most days on market. Tell them that you would be happy to list their home for $1 million! But it really doesn't do anybody any good if there is not a buyer to purchase it. An overpriced home will bounce buyers faster than a Ping-Pong ball. Go through the pros and cons of overpricing a home, and make sure to point out the majority of the cons! In reality, overpricing the home really does not do anybody any good. If

they decide to go with this option, don't leave that house until you have created a price-reduction plan for that home. Set the stage up front that you both agree to talk after ten days if there has not been any activity. The worst enemy when selling a home is days on market. Price it right.

OPTION TWO: Pricing the home at "fair market value." Let them know that this is the preferred option. Let's stick to what the market is dictating, what the market is telling us to do. We know and have statistical data as to what buyers are doing. We will have the highest chance of selling your home quickly and for fair market value when we stick to the prices that buyers are actually paying right now. We have the data that prove that if we stick to this price range, we will get your home sold. And again, start to point out the pros and cons, emphasizing the pros. This is going to be the preferred strategy!

OPTION THREE: Underpricing a home and *hopefully* create a bidding war. Now, let them know that there is risk involved in this, but every so often, we can actually get the bidding war up above what the market value of their home is. It is rare, it is possible, but it can cause headaches and feelings of being caught in a "bait-and-switch" scenario. We are professional real-estate agents. Everything we do must be in the best interest of the clients both buyers and sellers...not the agent!

Now, you know your market better than we do. Help them choose the pricing strategy that is going to be the best for them given the current market conditions. It is going to be different in every part of the United States! What happens in California is not the same as Idaho and so on.

Inevitably, the discussion always follows with, "Well, what do you charge?" What are your fees that I have to pay? Here is what we tell our clients: "We are worth ten percent without a doubt, but we only charge three percent for all we offer to you." Their eyes light up, they get excited, and they are on cloud nine! Assure them that you'll do everything, the professional photography, videography, aerial photography (if you're licensed to do so), market their home on over one hundred home-search sites, social media their home, Facebook live, open houses, and so on, and you only charge that 3 percent for your services. Confirm to them the incredible value they will receive by using you as their professional!

Then ask the seller, "Mr. seller, what do you feel we should compensate the buyer's agent who brings a buyer to your home?" You see, you just nailed *your* commission! Now we need to get the other agent paid. Always suggest that you offer him a 3 percent. The higher commission you offer the buyers' agents, the more motivated they're going to be to present their home as an option for their buyers with whom they are working with. As we reduce their commission (because we are *not* going to reduce ours), fewer and fewer agents will present it as an option to their buyers; agents feel they are worth the fee and sometimes just won't show it if they don't get their full commission. Now let him know that although you do not agree with the strategy of those buyers' agents who do not show a home because their commission is lower, unfortunately, it is the truth. So, the more generous we can be to a buyer's agent, the more likely we are going to be to sell your home. Although, the goal is for you to double side it anyway!

Point out the fact that as real-estate agents, we don't get paid until the home sells and that you have everything to gain by making it happen!

Make sure that the sellers feel like they're in the driver's seat the whole time. Influence them, and help them to understand the correct path to take for the sale of their home, but don't let them feel like they are being steered. Let them feel that they're in control and are making the decisions, but definitely coach them and help them to make the right decisions for selling their home. Remember to listen, resolve concerns, build the relationship of trust, and make them feel comfortable. Be yourself. Be professional and confident, but not overbearing and annoying. Catch them off guard! If you play the guitar, piano, or any instrument and you see one sitting over there in the corner, ask if you can play them a quick song! Let down your guard, get down on their level, and don't be afraid to be yourself in front of them. The more real you can be with them, the more you will connect with them, and the better the relationship of trust will be. We actually have a neat story about this in our academy about how an offer was accepted by playing a seller a song on the guitar. Check it out! True Story!

Now, just some quick reminders as you walk to their home, even if you have been through a similar floor plan two hundred times; always compliment them on their home, and be excited to see their home. Let them know what a wonderful job they have done with their home, even if it doesn't look that great! But also, don't be shy to make suggestions. If they have too much clutter in the home, tell them to remove it. Let them know that open spaces are what buyers want to see. By getting on their level in the beginning, letting down your guard, and building a relationship of trust, it will allow you to be open and more direct with them in your feedback that you have on preparing their home for listing.

Finally, at the end of the listing presentation, ask them for the business! Tell them you are ready to go to work for them. Let them know that you are anxious and excited to get their home sold, so much so that you have already started marketing their home! Make sure that you are enhancing their real-estate experience.

In Review:

- Always overdeliver, even when you aren't asked to.
- Invest in photography equipment (or people) who will make your listings stand out.
- Be on their level in the very beginning.
- Let down your guard and be friendly, building a relationship of trust.
- Be loving, but direct in your communication.
- Working with sellers can be tricky.
- Everything depends on you in their eyes.
- Earn their trust.
- Show them your skills.
- Actively work on your skills.

- Make sure to always be monitoring what your competition is doing.
  - Stay in regular contact.
    - Always overdeliver.

CHAPTER 9

CRAP! WHAT IF THE HOME DOESN'T SELL?

We've all been there. We give an awesome, confident presentation. We tell them how amazing and wonderful we are! We do all the things we promise, *except* getting their home sold! It happens to all of us! And there is nothing worse than a client being disappointed and frustrated with their agent. How do we face this opposition? How do we keep them happy? We have had to learn the hard way what works and what doesn't. And we have finally narrowed it down to a few techniques that have worked every time. In all these techniques, they are best explained to the client in person rather than over the phone. Show them you care enough to stop by their home and make a personal visit. Just this week, we had a client text us with some frustrations that their home wasn't selling. We immediately went over to their home, unannounced, and they were shocked! In fact, they were even brought to tears that I would take the time to go to their home and go over some strategies with them. Let them know you care and are taking initiative to get their home sold. In any case, let them know that they have the best marketing for their home for the area and that you are doing *all* the right things. Here are some strategies that you can work with them on:

Strategy 1:
The Three Reasons Why a Home Doesn't Sell

In this strategy, let the seller know that there are three things that sell a home. *Price, location,* and *condition.* Review the price with them. Go back to the recently sold homes that you reviewed with them in the listing appointment and double check that you are on par with what the market is doing. If you are a little high, suggest a price reduction. If the price is right on par, go to the next item. Location. How is the location of their home? Is it on a busy road? Is there anything negative about the home's location? How about the condition of the home? Does the price perhaps need to be adjusted to better reflect market conditions or the home condition? Ask if you can walk through their home again with them and check to make sure there isn't anything that got missed that should really be fixed, cleaned, or adjusted. How is the curb appeal? Is there anything they can do to enhance it? If everything checks out on all three, let them know that we might just need to be patient! The right buyer will come! Perhaps see if they will do a slight price reduction just to entice and motivate buyers. Explain to them that, by doing this, the online-search websites will generally send an e-mail out to all who have saved their home online. It will bring that home back to the top of the mind of interested buyers.

Strategy 2: Fresh Pictures

Sometimes people won't click on a house online because the main photo may not appeal to them or they already saw it and pass on it every other time they see it. Maybe there were a couple of pictures of the inside that didn't turn out the way they should have! Offer to come shoot some fresh photos, and upload those into the MLS, so people who may have passed over this home before won't initially recognize it! Sometimes we have to play these mind games with buyers. Freshening up the photos, reorganizing them, and changing the main-page photo can help get revive an old listing.

Strategy 3: Pull it off and Relist

If you have racked up days on market and you are starting to appear on the second or third page of home-search sites, pull the listing, wait twenty-four hours, and relist the home. This will put it back at the top of the search results, and it wouldn't hurt either to change a few of the photos of the house at this time. Keep in mind, when using this strategy, some home-search websites will not automatically reset the days on market. However, oftentimes you can call them or e-mail their customer support and let them know that it is a new listing and the days on market need to be reset.

Out of the three strategies we shared with you, the first strategy of the three reasons why a home isn't selling has been the most effective for us. More often than not, it just requires patience because, as a "prepared" agent, you will already have done all the right things and it is just a matter of waiting for the right buyer!

Now, if you have had a lot of activity and either no offers or really low offers, explain to the client that it is a clear indication that our price is too high. Generally, our first couple of offers are going to be the best offers! Not always, but generally because the real buyers, those who are qualified, ready, and willing are circling around like birds to check out the newest listing. These are your *ready* buyers! So sometimes a quick sale will happen. When that offer does come in, people know that if a home hasn't been on the market for very long that they cannot come in with a low ball. But, if multiple offers come in that are similarly low, it is a good indication that, for whatever reason (location or condition), buyers do not feel it is worth the list price, and they should adjust to meet the market.

More than anything, always make your seller aware that you are conscious of their home and are doing everything in your power to get it sold for them. Perhaps the entire neighborhood isn't selling! Let them know it isn't just their home! Keep them up to date with market statistics. You should be on the phone with your sellers, whether good news, bad news, or no news, and giving them updates. Stay in contact! Do not ever list a home and leave it to good luck! You can prevent upset clients all together if you just stay in touch with them and keep them in the loop. One of the biggest complaints we get when we work with people who had previously been listed with another agency is that the agent sticks a sign in the yard and wishes their way to the closing table, and they never hear or see from him or her again. Prove that you are better than that. Why? Because you *are* better than that!

Conclusion

The truth is, working with buyers and sellers can be tricky. Working with as many buyers and sellers as we do on an annual basis, we have learned what works, what doesn't, and how we can best serve those purchasing or selling a home. Now, this is just the surface. We cannot teach you in just one short book how to be the perfect real-estate agent. There are other factors that will come into play such as back-end business structure, how your brand is perceived by the general public, generating the leads to get the buyers and sellers, as well as time management. All these things and more are what we dive very deep into in the Real Estate Hustle Academy. We invite you to visit http://www.therealestatehustle.com to learn more about everything you'll gain by taking the real-estate academy course.

BONUS CHAPTER: CHAPTER 10
Resolving The Biggest Complaint in Real Estate

Survey after survey after survey has revealed one massive complaint among just about every real-estate agent in the industry. It is driving consumers out of their minds, driving down our value, making our big website competitors look better. But it is something you can fix and will fix, *today*! This *one* factor is going to make you incredibly successful in real estate, or it will make you drown like the rest. This is one you are going to want to pay attention to.

The biggest complaint in our industry and the gripe we always hear when we take over someone else's client but happens to be one of our biggest compliments we receive in our real-estate brokerage is *communication*! Time after time after time, we hear this complaint, especially when we take over someone else's client, an expired listing, or anybody who had previously worked with another agent. We always ask the buyers about their previous experience because, quite frankly, we love to learn from other agent's mistakes! Each and every time, the complaint is nearly identical. "Tom, the agent, promised us the moon when he listed our house, and then we never heard from him again." "I could never get my agent to answer her phone!" "I lost out on the home I wanted because my agent never called me back and I wanted to put in an offer."

So, what is the deal? Why are real-estate agents so terrible at communication? We know that answering our phone is going to bring us business, so why don't we do it? Why don't *you* do it? I recently submitted an offer on a home in a neighboring community, and when I called to present the offer, this agent didn't answer. Her mailbox was full. So, I e-mailed the offer over with a long explanation of our offer, backing our lower offer up with comparables, and essentially typed out our negotiations. But I never heard back! So, I proceeded to text the agent. No response. I gave it a few hours, never heard back, so I called. No answer. Voice mail still full. I kept trying and trying, and, *finally*, on the day that the seller had to give us a response, she texted me and said, "The sellers are going to need another day." I'm pretty sure that was code for, "I totally didn't know about your offer because I am a terrible communicator." Another day went by. No word from the agent. Called her. Voice mail *still* full. We waited another day. I called her, and she texted back, "Sellers need another day." We gave them one more day, which we really shouldn't have, and I called, no answer, voice mail still full, she texted back, "Sellers are going to need one more day." We moved on to another home. This was a chance that the agent could have gotten this home sold for these clients. Our offer was slightly low, but we know she didn't do any negotiating with them, so who knows if she even talked to them? The lack of communication to us turned us off, and we moved on to more homes.

Nothing frustrates us more than dealing with agents like this. And it is unfortunate for the seller! Maybe this is similar to how you operate your business currently. If so, we are going to repent and change your ways today! But we get it! It is easy to do. Phone calls roll in each and every day. It can get *very* overwhelming. And if we have had a particularly bad day, we don't really feel like talking to anybody! The struggle is real, and without a system to handle communication, especially incoming communication, our lives can easily be taken over to the point that we stop answering our phone, which, in our industry, is the quickest way to reduce our value and the quickest way to lose business like the agent I was just referring to demonstrated.

We are going to set you up for success with your communication. This is easy to master. Anybody can do it. It just takes dedication and persistence. But the results will be incredible. We are going to go through the ways you need to be communicating with your prospects, how to capture more and more of them, how to communicate with your buyers during a transaction, with your sellers during a transaction, and post-transaction communication for both the buyer and seller.

Remember, people want to believe in your brand and feel that they belong to your community. This shouldn't be just another real-estate transaction for them. This needs to be an experience! Something great and positively memorable! We focus much of our real-estate business on the experience our clients receive from us! And let me tell you where that came from.

I love to learn from other businesses. I am fascinated by other people's success and do everything I can to learn from them. A few years ago, my wife and I were driving back to Idaho from California. I wanted to surprise her and stay in Trump Hotel in Las Vegas as an early birthday present. We were young and had never stayed in a five-star hotel before, and I just wanted to spoil her.

Our four-hour drive from Southern California to Las Vegas turned into nine hours after a massive accident shut the entire freeway down in the middle of the desert. It was literally a parking lot. I was so upset. Now, up to this point, she thought that we were going to stay in a Motel 6 in Vegas. I told her that because I really wanted this to be a surprise. I had spent a lot of money on this room and was getting so frustrated that we were hardly going to get to enjoy it!

Well, we finally rolled into Vegas, pulled up to the Trump Hotel, and not only was she shocked, but I was blown away. The professionalism you experience there is unmatched! Someone came out and greeted us in our vehicle and helped us to unload our luggage. When we walked in, the front-desk clerk didn't just wait for us behind the desk. He greeted us in the lobby, gave us a very warm welcome, and, after he checked us in, walked us and the bellboy to the elevator. Very different from a normal hotel stay. As we arrived at our room, the bellboy stayed until we could look at the room and make sure we were 100 percent satisfied.

Every time we needed something, we were greeted by [name]. It was as if they had known us for years! And you have to hand it to their team for their bold move of opening a hotel in Las Vegas *without* a casino! That was a bold move indeed! But they were targeting the experience of the client. After our experience in this hotel, I knew that we had to offer the same experience in our real-estate business. The Trump Hotel was above and beyond with their communication skills, making sure we were happy with every aspect of our visit, and you could tell that they put a lot of time and effort into your experience. They have won awards for their customer service! I kept thinking that this is how I want our business to run!

Knowing that communication and customer service are the biggest complaints in real estate, we brainstormed on how we can make real estate a five-star experience. We were going to solve the communication problems in real estate once and for all. By doing so, we knew that just that alone would put us light years ahead of our competition! So, we created the Five Points to Break the Communication Standard. It is a simple, effective, and a mostly automated formula to stay in excellent communication with your prospects, buyers, and sellers. This is very important information, so be sure to pay attention and take good notes on this! We are going to walk you through setting up "drip systems" for each of your clients, the why behind it, and you are going to see immediate results!

So, let's jump right into the five points. Remember to take notes on this!

Point 1: Keep communication short, sweet, and simple. This is going to ring especially true with your e-mail marketing. You do not want to flood your clients or prospects with long, boring e-mails! Or long and boring phone calls. Let them know what they need to know, cut out the fluff, and don't think that more is better! As you set people up on your drip systems, they are going to be far less likely to unsubscribe from your drip system if you send them short, concise, friendly e-mails. Think of Twitter, for example. You have to keep everything under 140 characters to get your message out. It forces you to be creative! Be the Twitter of communication! On the note of your e-mail marketing, some agents are big into HTML e-mails that look fancy. Sure, they look great, but after extensive research by professional marketers, they have found that people delete those e-mails quicker because they identify them as *spam*, or they actually get caught in the spam filters on e-mails. A plain-text e-mail is exactly what you want to send them. It is more personal, they think you sat down and wrote it, and the likelihood of them reading it is much higher.

Point 2: Communicate often, whether they are a prospect, buyer, seller, or past client; stay in regular communication with them. And let me tell you, we have never heard the complaint, "My Realtor communicates too much with me!" During this stressful time for a buyer and seller, there is never too much communication.

Point 3: Keep it relevant, and keep your communication relevant to the people you are working with. Let them know things that they need to know. Forget the recipe cards or digital newsletters. Honestly, the majority of people could care less about reading those! Sorry! If they are prospects, keep them informed with the market. If they are buyers, keep them informed with all the steps of the transaction. If they are sellers, keep them informed about showings or progress with a current buyer!

Point 4: Video is no longer an option—*it's a must*! You want to know the best way to keep people engaged in you and your brand? Talk to them! Let them see your face! Get in front of them even when you physically cannot be in front of them. Video is such a powerful tool that you absolutely need to be utilizing. We will show you how to get this set up because you are going to have to record several of these!

Point 5: Texting is no longer an option—*it's a must*! Remember, we are working with a lot of millennials. And the older generations are adopting the ways of this generation. I bet you can probably count on one hand the number of people that you have recently met that don't text. Everybody does it, and it is one of the most popular forms of communication now! E-mails are still powerful, phone calls are still powerful, but texting blows them out of the water! Here are some incredible statistics on text messages. Ninety-eight percent of all text messages are opened. Only 20–30 percent of e-mails are opened. More people have access to mobile phones than toilets! Ninety-seven percent of Americans text. Ninety-five percent of texts are read within three minutes of sending. These statistics are *unbelievable*!

There you have it! These five points are going to change the way you run your entire business! No matter the size of your real-estate company, you need to be automating as much of your communication as possible. This will save hours and hours of your precious time and will make you so powerful in your real-estate career. Literally, with these five points, you can change the entire face of your business, win more clients, and convert more leads to sales!

www.ingramcontent.com/pod-product-compliance
Lightning Source LLC
Chambersburg PA
CBHW070925220526
45472CB00014B/365